My Fc

All Material

This book is the reflection of my personal relationship with the Lord Jesus Christ. I want people to read how His Word influences my thoughts and ideas. He is a never-ending spring and the source of my strength since I was a young girl and He can be your's too. These are my poems written from the year 2000-2017. Poetry has been my form of expression that God has given me to share my story. I hope you enjoy it. He loves you and wanted me to tell you that you are precious in His sight. Jesus is the way, the truth and the life no man comes to the Father but through Him. Accept Him in you heart so that you may have eternal life.

This book is designed to be
shared, not to be kept forever.
As you read this you will be
on a tour of my mind.
Buckle your seat belts and enjoy
the ride.
MAY THE LORD RICHLY BLESS
YOU!!!

Angelica Yanet Sanchez

This Book is Dedicated to My Mom

Maria del Refugio Enriquez Aldaz

My Beautiful Mother

She is a cook like no other
She loves flowers and birds
The birds also love her
She was made by my Heavenly Father
Who decided I would be privileged to be her
daughter
She taught me not to care what people think
If she saw something in the trash that she liked
She'd go and pick it up
She worked hard like a man
But is also as soft as a rose petal
Roses are her favorite flower
Especially the ones that belonged to my
Grandmother
Yellow and purple are her favorite colors
Bless Her Lord
I am a reflection of my beautiful Mother

*** 7/25/1953 - 5/12/2016 ***

I want to thank my Lord and Savior
*****Jesus Christ*****

For making this book possible and being so patient with me. I will never stop thanking you for my Life, I love you Father.

I also want to thank my Husband

Daniel Sanchez

For loving me with all my imperfections and pushing me to get this book done. You're the best husband in the world my gorgeous love.

I also want to Thank my Pastors

Eddie and Rosa Figueroa

For preaching the Truth to me and helping me to get to this point in my life.

Lastly I want to thank my children, family and friends that have been there for me.

***I LOVE YOU All ***

Remember that Jesus loves you more

I Think

Therefore I know

That Jesus Christ

Is King and Lord

Romans 1:18-20

"For God's wrath is revealed from heaven against all godlessness and unrighteousness of people who by their unrighteousness suppress the truth, since what can be known about God is evident among them, because God has shown it to them. For His invisible attributes, that is, His eternal power and divine nature, have been clearly seen since the creation of the world, being understood through what He has made. As a result, people are without excuse. For though they knew God, they did not glorify Him as God or show gratitude. Instead, their thinking became nonsense, and their senseless minds were darkened."

From the Heart

Too many things to think about
I don't know where to start
I should examine what's going on in my head
I'm scared, but I don't know of what
Maybe it's when I go to sleep on my bed
My mind gets lost inside my head
There's a puzzle in my head
I try to solve it, but give up instead
Maybe I should wait GOD will be a while
He has a lot of people to worry about
He picks me up when I fall down
I can't explain the love He has for me
They say it's big enough to fill the sea
Maybe I need to flee because the love He has is too
good for me
Sometimes I can't see, but He's pursuing me
He has to get me before I can show someone else
You have to be taught before you can go and teach
it yourself
How do I spread the word "The Lord is always
around"

He wants you to follow Him
Don't worry about the when, where, why, how
He has the answer to any question you have in
your head
Amazing, I know
Maybe we should all try to get to know Him more
If you do you will see the undying love He has for
you and for me
The Lord will never let us down, He never fails
No matter what He will prevail
Lord help me be loving caring and kind
Help me be like you Lord, it might take some time
Be patient with me LORD, I'm only human you
know
With time, I'm sure I will be refined
By allowing you to work in my mind
My goal is to be with the LORD
there's no telling how far I have to go
On the quest for the Love that is hard find
I WILL DEFINITELY TRY...

Psalms 139:3

"You comprehend my path
and my lying down, and are acquainted
with all my ways."

Gunshots

Gunshots
That's what I heard
But it was like no one said a word
Like they all knew we were about to be served
That night the sound of death was heard
They did a terrible deed for a bad cause indeed
LORD, why do people feel that need?
Or feel as though they have control over the world?
LORD, they robbed me of the happiness I had nicely
put away
In a matter of seconds I realized things were never
going to be the same
I hate living in this world now I just wait
My thoughts just swirl around my head as I lay in
bed
I know the LORD has things under control
He's never wrong
He's the one that decides if my life will be long
Why do people try to act like GOD?
Their mind is full of fog
LORD; clear my mind of devilish thoughts

I don't ever want to be responsible for the tears of
someone's family
That night LORD there was a horrible tragedy!
LORD, I know you know who did this
Tell him that;
"My kids needed their Daddy desperately
you took their Daddy away from them
what you did was cowardly!"
I can't explain why you would do such a thing
If I would of done what you did
I could not live with myself
So how could you manage to even look at yourself?
I forgive you for what you did
because ahead lay a dark destiny
tortured by the demons you will be

I pray you ask for forgiveness from the King
Now I just wait for GOD to grant justice for me

Psalms 1:6

"For the LORD watches over the way
of the righteous, but the way of the wicked
leads to ruin."

My Testimony

The assassination of Rene
It occurred in August on the 10th day
The day my man was assassinated in front of our
face
The killer just came up to our car
He shot Rene at point blank range
I just remember that the first bullet was like an
explosion
And as soon as the smoke cleared away
the killer was standing right in front of Rene's face
I could not see him cause he had a hoody to hide his
face
I remember there was glass everywhere
That is when I realized Rene had been shot
The killer just walked away
This was obviously not his first time
Killing someone face to face
Me, not realizing that Rene was not okay
I remember telling him "Rene, drive away"
He tried to save our life that day
He was already drifting away

As Rene turned on the car and put his foot on the
gas
the killer turned around and started walking back
towards us
Firing another bullet
Straight to the front windshield
When I saw him coming back my first instinct was
to duck
I just remember hearing our car getting shot up
The thought that ran through my head was
"I guess this is the end"
When I looked up
I saw that Rene was shot in his face
If I wouldn't of ducked that would of been my end
I remember thinking
I can't die today
This is my testimony
The Lord saved our lives that day
Even though I wish sometimes that I too should of
died
It's harder now to be alive
EVERYDAY
I think about what took place

At that moment, time and place...

One thing you must remember is that my two
children
were in the back seat
we all suffered because of what this person did
But we know that God will grant us justice
he will suffer for making us cry...Unless He repents
Listen to what I said
and make your decision today
don't wait till something horrible happens to
acknowledge God
He is the best thing that can happen to you...

Plus He loves you!

Psalms 37:39

"The salvation of the righteous is from the LORD,
their refuge in a time of distress."

My Life

In my life I've seen a lot of things
Good, bad, some things were so horrific
That no human being should ever see
The death of your love one
With his brain splattered all over the front seat
I've learned a lot from that
One, appreciate those around you
Two, life is not a walk in the park
Three. Always show your emotions
You never know whom you can help
By not being shy to share yourself
My life is a testimony that even though you
backslide
God still has mercy and wants to be by your side
So don't reject His love for you
He stopped at nothing to pay the toll for you
So like I said...

In my life I've seen a lot of things....

Jeremiah 3:22

"Return, you faithless children. I will heal your unfaithfulness. "Here we are, coming to You, for You are the LORD our God."

Walk With Me

I'll never forget how you made me feel
That love was real
I want everyone to know how I felt when you made
my heart melt
I knelt on my knees and thanked the LORD
For a love like yours
I just thought a love like ours would last
Now I have to put you in the past
Even though I think about you in the present
I never forget your essence
You'll be in my heart forever
You were always so clever
I know that death is inevitable
Walk with me I want to tell you a story
Of a life that I lived once
It was too good to be true
I didn't even get to enjoy the glory
I remember the time I lost it all
I didn't want to let it go
Good things only last for a moment
All you can do is treasure and hold it
In your heart, mind and spirit
Somebody had to kill it!!!!!!

Watch out for envious people
They're quick to take it cause they can't make it
They'll plot to kill or plan to steal from you
Not knowing they're on a short road to hell
God doesn't like you trying to go and kill people
yourself
They keep drinking the devil's drink
So they're going to mingle with devilish creeps
They have no light in there spirit
The devil try's to eclipse the LORD with all the
sinning'
It's in your power to say:
"devil leave me alone!!!"
"I want to go back home to my father"
"He'll never send me to slaughter
The devil's just after your soul
he'll never console
he wants to break the mold made in the image of
the LORD
Just call on JESUS He'll come to your rescue
Believe me, it's true
There's nothing He can't do
He'll make you new
Angie came to spit game
To all the males and the dames

17

I use to be out for fame
now I just want to speak in JESUS name
I think we should all be on the same page
Are you going with the Lord?
Or are you going the opposite way?
That's the question I ask you today
Repent for your sins or your going to go to a very
dark place
Where you'll never see God's grace
and everyone's got evil written all over there face
You'll disappear without a trace
You won't catch anyone smiling
Because it's not a happy place
Once your there there's no turning back
So think about the decision you make
It determines your fate
Don't wait
Think straight
Take action, it' time to recuperate
The Lord's known for healing and dealing with this
life full of strife
Don't think twice
Wake up this is life
Or you'll be swimming in a lake of lava
Wishing you had a father
The devil will be winning as long as you are sinning

Listen to my story
And Give GOD all the Glory
Enough is enough!
People are stuck on all this worldly stuff
Don't take what I say as a bluff
It's time to emancipate
Put GOD first and things will turn out great
Overwhelmed with pain
I feel like I'm going insane
But, hey I can't complain
I cried a cup full of tears
Take a drink and you'll feel the pain
It's unbelievable this Love I feel
I miss the way you would caress my face
But I know now, your in God's grace
You took your love away
You can never be replaced
So rest in Peace, now your in a better place
Where everything is golden, shinny and new
Who would of knew?
They say there's a heaven
Well it's true!
Let's stop being a bunch of fools
always breaking all the rules
Please listen to my story
These are all things I've been through

My Babies

Lalo and Sonia
I am your eyes
I am here to tell you...
How much your Daddy loved you
while he was alive
The way he bit your little fingers till you cried
How he was so happy when you were born
He was there all the way with no delays
But he could not stay
We must not argue with the Lord
He knows what is in store
He is no longer here but we still miss him like before
No matter how much time passes by
I will still wonder why...
Beautiful was the love we had for each other
I felt how much he loved me when he hugged me
It was all so lovely
A masterpiece
Painted in time

The love between you and I...

Working Mother

I am a working mother
Even though my kids don't have their father
I feel like were going to make it
God's got us covered
Everyday we have food to eat and
Every night we have somewhere to sleep
I thank the LORD for my everyday things
For being able to wake up and be next to my kids
Lord, I cant thank you enough for everything
you've done
Since I was born you put breath in my lungs
I'm here on earth
Smiling, Laughing, Having fun
Lord, I thank you for everyone
I thank you for all the times I've had
Some happy
Some sad
Even the times when I was mad
I feel more in control than before
I just sit back and watch the show
I don't get angry anymore
I love me more
I can forgive more easily
Thank you LORD

My Thoughts

My thoughts are like birds
They start of as eggs
Those then become chicks
That soon find there way out of the shell
Once they are out of the shell
They get fed and grow
Next they are ready to fly away
Off they go....
There is no specific place
Because the sky is such a big space...

Colossians 3:1-2

"So if you have been raised with the Messiah, seek
what is above, where the Messiah is, seated at the
right hand of God. Set your minds on what is
above, not on what is on the earth."

God will Bring You Through

God has brought me through the hard times
Now I am living the good times
Keep the faith and focus on Him
He will deliver you from the hands of your enemies
Can't you see?
He is always there for me
The proof is right before your eyes
So when times get tough
Bend your knees and pray to the one up above
He will answer your petition
According to His mercy and Love
Let Him be your refuge
He can protect you with His mighty hand
He promises that He will never leave you or
forsake you
For it is written:
"The Lord hears the needy
and does not despise his captive people"
Psalms 69 verse 33
Lord, you do so much for me
Thank you for my family
We could of died
But You kept us alive
Thank you for loving me

You were right there for us
Your angels you sent
They hovered over us
That is why right here you see me
All because you never had forgotten me
Even though I put You to the side
And I didn't keep on trying
You showed me you're not like me
There is none mightier than He
From my God
All my enemies will flee
He will keep His promises
His word is true and full of knowledge
Wisdom, Understanding and Love
For God is Love
There is no love without God
Can't you understand?
You can't live without Him
He is the answer
To all your questions
The remedy that your heart needs
Give your life to Him
He just wants us to trust Him
His Holy Spirit will guide us
Though there will be thunderstorms
God will give you peace
You will sleep right through it

We must also serve Him
For He is worthy
of all your praise
His only son's life He laid
Slain was He
On the 3rd day He had rose
He put an end to the eternal death we faced
That was our price to pay
He took it upon himself
His life He gave
For you and for me

1 Thessalonians 4:14

"Since we believe that Jesus died and rose again, in the same way God will bring with Him those who have fallen asleep through Jesus."

Trying To Understand

It is hard to understand God
Because it was not meant for us to understand Him
But for us to be in awe of His Glory
And to praise Him for it
It is so deep that we can't understand
The capacity of His mighty hands
So DON'T try to understand
Just lift up your hands
And give Him the honor that He deserves
For the things that He does that you can't even
grasp

Ecclesiastes 8:16-17

"I tried to understand all that happens on earth. I
saw how busy people are, working day and night
and hardly ever sleeping. I also saw all that God
has done. Nobody can understand what God does
here on earth. No matter how hard people try to
understand it, they cannot. Even if wise people say
they understand, they cannot; no one can really
understand it."

Honey

God made honey
so you and I can see
How sweet His love is
For you and for me
To be honest
His love is even sweeter
Nothing can compare
To how much He really cares for us....
He tells me everyday
How special I am in so many ways
After all I am the work of His mighty hands
He wants me to display my talents to glorify Him
I say why not?
He is worthy of my praise!
I will lift Him high
Can I get an AMEN!!!

Psalms 34:8

"Taste and see that the LORD is good.
How happy is the man who takes refuge in Him!"

Wind Chimes

The wind chimes give the wind a voice
so you can hear how the Lord moves amongst us
The wind is something you can feel but you can't
see
Just like my Lord
It is a mystery amongst many other things
For it is written in:
Psalms 19 verses 1 through 4
"The heavens declare the glory of God
and the skies proclaim the works of His hands,
Day after day the pour forth speech
Night after night
they display knowledge.
There is no speech or language
where there voice is not heard
There voice goes out into all the earth
their words to the end of the world..."
It is the language of God
Too holy to understand
Also to majestic to capture
Just like the wind...

My Prayers

My prayers come from within my soul
When I pray, I pray to God himself
He hears me and answers my petitions
Everyday God loves when we speak to Him
We have access to the Most Holy Place
Through the blood of Jesus when we accept Him
In there is where I enter when I pray
The curtain was torn when Jesus died for my sin
Now there is nothing stopping me from talking to
the Lord
I pray for my enemies and I pray for my friends
I pray that my loved ones will get to know Him
I pray for salvation for those around me
I also pray to stay strong in Him that sustains me
When we pray we are spending time with Him
We are letting Him know that we love Him
We are acknowledging Him
When I pray to God
I am talking to my best friend
He knows everything
Yet He loves it when I tell Him
From my own words how my day has been
How I saw His beauty everywhere that I went
So please take the time to talk to Him
Because every knee will bow before Him

The Mastermind

Lord,
The thought of You
Your Glory, Might, Splendor
Magnificence
is too much for the human mind
That is why I want to take the time to Thank You
For all that you have made,
For my viewing pleasure
The Stars in the sky
The birds in the air
The sun, the moon
All this my mind can't consume
There is not enough room
Your countless wonders
You are the definition of beauty
Your superior intelligence
That surpasses all
You are God,
Like you there is no other
You gave us so much to discover
And everything screams.
"I was made by my Heavenly Father."
"I COULD NOT OF EVOLVED
I WAS DESIGNED BY A MASTERMIND!"

Roots

We are all like trees
None of us are the same
First of all
We all have our own roots
Some go deep into the ground
Others are closer to the top
Sometimes we forget from where we came
Depending on your roots
That's how good your tree will look
Your stump, when cut open can be read like a book
That keeps track of things that took place
Without you being able to erase
It is a trace
Some will grow really tall
and produce delicious fruit
While others end up with no fruit
Their tree is dry
Since they never took the time to know their
Creator
Which means we depend on a relationship with The
Most High to be healthy trees
If not we will end up lonely as can be
Stuck in the corner where the sun has not shown
because they have not known....
Elohim

No Matter What

Lord,
Whatever the circumstances I have to face
Your direction is the one I will take
I will learn from my mistakes
I am thankful for everything you gave
That was the ultimate sacrifice
Nothing else can compare
Of this I am aware
The price you paid will not be in vain
Only my heavenly Father gave up His only son to
be slain
For my sin
To you Lord, thanks I give
Because of you I have learned to forgive
As well as to live my life serving you
And those you send my way
Thank you!!!!
I love you....

For My Friends

I want the best for you
Because you're my friend
I just wish you know that I care for you
And Jesus really loves you
I know life is not fair
We will go through aches and pain
There will be plenty of rain
Just don't be afraid
God will be there for you
Remember it has to start with you
Don't you know that Jesus is a gentleman?
He won't barge in on you
He needs to be invited
Only then can He dine with you
Don't wait another day
His Salvation is a gift for you
His blood He had to shed for you to receive....
Everlasting life
Remember
Only you can deny yourself this blessing

Revelation 3:20

"Listen! I stand at the door and knock. If anyone
hears My voice and opens the door, I will come
in to him and have dinner with him,
and he with Me."

I Will Defend

Lord Jesus,
I will defend your Holy name
I will tell people of your majesty
As well as how You had mercy on me
God, you are so good to me
You've given me the victory
I am no longer blind
I can see
You are always with me
Yet I cannot count the blessings you've given to me
Writing a book would not be enough to tell of your
wonders....

Mark 5:18-19

"As He was getting into the boat, the man who had been demon-possessed kept begging Him to be with Him. But He would not let him; instead, He told him, "Go back home to your own people, and report to them how much the Lord has done for you and how He has had mercy on you."

Firm

I don't sway like the waves
I stand firm like a tree
I am planted by the water, which is why my leaves
are always green
Lord you're the reason
it is always a beautiful season
Nothing can get me down as long as I have you
He helps me to get through all kinds of stuff
Believe me, sometimes it gets rough
Don't let your troubles let you forget where you are
firmly planted
As well as who you put your faith in
Always remember Jesus loves you

Jeremiah 17:8

"He will be like a tree planted by water: it sends its
roots out toward a stream, it doesn't fear when
heat comes, and its foliage remains green. It will
not worry in a year of drought or cease producing
fruit."

Treated Like A Lady

You always treat me like a lady
It makes me think that maybe
You might be ready for a girl like me
I hope you see
A girl like me is hard to please
And I see your willing to give it a shot
So I say "why not?"
Let's have the kind of relationship everyone is
jealous of
We'll make all jaws drop
then we can't be stopped
We've accelerated on a fast trip to happiness
And I have everything I need
Jesus, My Children, You
So come on lets go
Let's not wait one minute more
You make my heart soar
to a place I have not been before

Lord,
Please bless our home
you've sent me a man that will be with me through
the storm
I no longer mourn

Thank you Lord!!
I can't express the joy I feel inside my soul
You've given me much more than I ever expected
See good things do happen
Even to the misfortunate
Before I watched every one be happy
I waited patiently
And your the one the Lord sent to me
Please don't rush into things
Let things just unfold on their own
If it's meant to be, it will be
Thank you Lord for the second chance you've given
me...

Psalms 30:11

"You turned my lament into dancing; You removed
my sackcloth and clothed me with gladness,"

Refine Me

Lord, refine me
With your magnificent mind
Do your work in me so I can do mine
I know you
All the time, everyday
We grow closer
Our relationship gets stronger
You are too awesome for me to ignore
With you is my reward

Revelations 22:12

"And, behold, I come quickly; and my
reward is with me, to give every man according as
his work shall be."

Dear Lord,

I know you hear my prayers
I thank you for worrying about all my cares
You are the perfect Father
Your love you shed on me
I cannot comprehend
All your mighty powers
I think about your perfect love
Along with all your mercy
That even though I fail you, you continue to love
me
Why Father?
I do not feel worthy of your great majesty
The King of Kings
The Lord of Lords
Is also a father to me
I pray for the world to accept you
Your free gift of eternal love
For all the people in the whole face of the earth
You saw our worth
Lord why can't they see?
That Jesus died for them and for me
I cannot imagine how You feel when a soul gets lost
Since with the blood of Jesus we were bought
The price was already paid

Your Son did not die in vain
How your heart must hurt
When you want to give people your love and
they just turn away
I want to tell the world
That your love has always been there
All they have to do is believe
In the blood of Jesus that was shed at Calvary
It cleans us even whiter than snow
I have not seen a white that white
But I will when I pass from this life
Unless you come for us first
Then I will get to dwell in the presence of your
glory FOREVER
But wait there's more
I will also get to be with the ones that passed before
My little girl is up there waiting for me!
As well as with the rest of my friends and family
That chose to accept you in there heart
That choice also comes with a golden crown
Made of the purest gold
That never needs to be polished
it's shine will never get old
OH how happy I will be
These are all promises from the Lord
I believe every single one

You too can have the hope of these things to come
When this life is done

Sarah, I miss you and can't wait to come home
Even though you can't be here with me
I know you are with God having fun
God's grace is enough for me
He gives me peace
OH what a wonderful God is He
Father I love thee....
Your daughter Angelica

James 1:12

"A man who endures trials is blessed, because when
he passes the test he will receive the crown of life
that God has promised to those who love Him."

Sarah

I did not know that when you said goodbye
That it would be the last time I would see you alive
I feel so bad for not taking better care of you
You were our precious gift from God himself
I should have taken more advantage of the time we
had together
The thought of you getting hit by her car hurts my
heart
I can't imagine what you felt
I am so sorry my mommas, I let you out of my sight
How stupid of me! Please forgive me!
You were such a good little baby to me
You were so smart
The most intelligent lil' lady
I was amazed at all your abilities
You praised God like and angel from heaven
Now I get it!
When you played your xylophone, it was so angelic
I will never forget how you would clean up your
own messes
When you would bring me the phone when it would
ring
How you would throw away the trash when it was
time to clean
When you pooped you would bring me a diaper

When I sneezed you would say "God bless you"
When you would wake you would yell and that
meant "Mommy I'm up"
I miss just looking at you with your hair all over
your face
How you would be greedy with your daddy and
wouldn't share him with me
There are no words to express how much we miss
you
We are happy you are in heaven
at the same time sad cause you are not here with us
Tell God I need some painkillers for my heart
I feel like my heart is bleeding
it hurts like no other pain I ever felt
Nothing can compare to this I have to face
The death of my little girl was never expected
But then again who expects for their loved ones to
die?
Lord, help me to cope with the loss of my child
I need your strength more than ever before
I trust in you Father
I will continue doing so more and more...

1 Thessalonians 4:13

"We do not want you to be uninformed, brothers,
concerning those who are asleep, so that you will
not grieve like the rest, who have no hope."

My Little Baby Girl

The thoughts and memories of you can fill the sea
I know that with us on earth you can never be
But I have the hope that one day I will get to see
your beautiful face again
When that day comes
From me you will never part
We've loved you from the start
Even though you are not here
The beautiful wonderful memories of you
From our hearts will never flee
Never, ever will you be forgotten
I know that God will take good care of you for your
Daddy and Me
Your soul is a beautiful masterpiece
From God's very own thoughts
How wonderful it must be for you to be in heaven
Even though here on earth we will never
understand why you had to die
I do not hate God for taking you away from me
He has a perfect plan
Plus He knows what happened throughout all the
land
He knows my sorrow
I will always wait for tomorrow
Hoping I am one day closer to you

Please Lord continue to give us the strength
to carry on
You know how much Sarah meant to her
Daddy and me
Lord, we miss her desperately
Her smile, hugs and kisses
She can never be replaced
Her spirit everywhere left a trace
Of a gorgeous little girl, with perfect curls
She brought so much joy to our world
Her laughter that filled the air
She made us forget about all our cares
Lalo and Sonia miss you too!
They miss chasing you
Your smile was like the sun always so bright
You were our shiny ray of light
Now our days don't seem as bright
I know you are making God laugh
Since you are so funny
He made you that way
That is why we enjoyed your presence every day....
We will always miss you lil' lady...
We will patiently wait till we see you again

Psalms 28:7
"The LORD is my strength and my shield; my
heart trusts in Him, and I am helped. Therefore my
heart rejoices, and I praise Him with my song."

Prayer For My Brother

Dear Lord,
I pray that you watch over my brother
I know if I ask you will make sure he is okay
This is something I want you to do for me everyday
He is in a place where bad things happen
And your the specialist who can shield him from all
harm
So I won't be alarmed
I know he is safe in your arms...
Thank you Lord For my brother Jesus

You are so good
I will always trust you....

Proverbs 3:5

"Trust in the LORD with all your heart, and do not
rely on your own understanding;"

Happy Day

Oh happy day
When we see the light
When we will no longer have to fight
Where you'll never have to worry about paying for
the light
Where we will no longer cry
For things that mean nothing at all
When we will no longer die
Where everything you see is happy and pleasant
Where it's never cold
where there is only the warmth of the LORD
Where there is no such thing as a storm
Where there is no such thing as the word mourn
When everyone wants to praise the Lord
There is no place for the devil in God's home
Where we will never feel alone
A place we can really call home
Where there is no such thing as a drought
Where you'll never feel doubt
I don't think I will ever figure out what life is all
about...

Revelation 21:23

"The city does not need the sun or the moon to shine
on it, because God's glory illuminates it, and its
lamp is the Lamb."

The News

What's going on in the news today?
That's what everyone wants to know
Well, people are dying
Children are crying
It's all a big struggle
We have so many things to juggle
Work, School, friends, family, boyfriends
There is always somewhere to attend
The things I am saying just can't be explained
Neurotransmitters are sending messages to my
brain
Some people don't even 10% of their brain
The thoughts are just flowing out
I know, it's insane
The things that go on in my head
People can't comprehend
I'm the Van Gogh of the lyrical flows
I will paint you a masterpiece
with the things that I speak
Don't get mad at me
This is my God given technique
So don't attempt to compete
You'll wound up getting beat.....

My soul gives praise only to My King

Talk To People

Talk to people
you never know what kind of heavy load is buried
deep inside their soul
Sometimes the things they do, they can't control
They do it cause they really want to cry
But can't stand for people to ask why
The things people do
Well, it reflects what they feel inside
I know this because I've witnesses it many times
I want to be a psychologist and study peoples minds
And see what makes them tic
You never know what you might find
You might find the light that makes them shine
Or you might find a dark place
Where they try to hide
People have been trying to figure out the human
mind for a very long time
I think they will keep searching
But they will never find
Sometimes our understanding isn't enough
to understand all this stuff
Leave it to a greater being
Lord, We don't understand all the things that
we're seeing....

The Body In Which We Reside

The body is the vessel of the soul
it doesn't work if the soul is not in it
If you think about it
the body is the capsule
The soul is the strings
And God is the one that allows the strings move

Because in Him we move and have our being
Without Him we could not do a thing...

Acts 17:28

"For in Him we live and move and exist, as even
some of your own poets have said, 'For we are also
His offspring."

The Creator

The one that gave the scent to a rose
that only the nose can expose
You give life to all those young and old
Tell me what needs to be told
So people can behold
Lord, within me I feel your presence
that can't be denied
Yahweh makes me feel like I can fly
Like a bird I soar through the sky

For you is all the Honor and Glory

I recognize it is You that allowed me to be alive

Isaiah 42:5

"This is what God, Yahweh, says-- who created the heavens and stretched them out, who spread out the earth and what comes from it, who gives breath to the people on it and life to those who walk on it--"

Help Me Father

Help me Father
To not listen to what the devil has to say
he will always try to be in my ear
Trying to make me go the wrong way
Help me to tune him out
So its only you I hear
Steer me
In your paths
Teach me in your ways
Feed me with your word everyday

John 6:35

"I am the bread of life," Jesus told them. "No one who comes to Me will ever be hungry, and no one who believes in Me will ever be thirsty again."

The Quest

I'm searching for the Lord
I don't have to go far because it's at my front door
And in everything I encounter as I explore
I'm on my way to place of no return
I don't know my way there but I'm sure
There will be signs that I can follow
I'm off to see if I can find some answers to some
questions that I have in my head
if I come back I'll share my findings
And my many discoveries
There are a lot of things I want to know
How can I explore the brain of the Lord?
He knows everything there is to know
LORD, I would like for You to show me the way
The devil tries to hold me back from your path
I say "NO, leave me alone!"
he throws a lot of things at me that got me running
for cover
he'll soon discover that I'll never belong to him
The Lord will always reign over my heart
If you feel empty inside
The LORD will fill that up in no time
He's always knocking at our Door
Go see who it is, it might change how you live

I'll Forgive You

Even if you're my best friend
and you betray me
I'll forgive you
Even if you turn me over to my enemies
I'll forgive you
Even if you say I am a worse than a murderer
I'll forgive you
Even if my life lies in your hands and
you decide to end it
Because I tried to show you what was right
I'll forgive you
No mater what you do I will forgive you
Your not going to stand between
my God and I
This is the reason why
His love is far to great for me to give it up
for a simple grudge
that will rot my very being
It will make me stop believing
I don't know if your seeing
what I am trying to get at
here's something that might help you understand
that
Forgiving your enemy is like burning hot coals on
his head and placing a blessing on thee....

Peace Like A River

The place in which I reside
must have one thing
the peace of the Lord inside
A place where my flesh and my spirit dwell
outside evil can run wild
but my place is where I can run and hide
it is my shelter from all bad weather
at night my dreams are sweet

In my place I feel mellow and relaxed
whether it is a messy or clean
my place still feels serene
It feels like there is a river right next to my door
and the sound of the water
makes my thoughts run out like a stream
In my place my ideas are born and start to grow
then unfold
cause my house is not a house
it is the place I call home

1 Peter 3:11

*"...and he must turn away from evil
and do what is good.
He must seek peace and pursue it,"*

Don't Eat the Forbidden Fruit

God took Adam and Eve and put them in the
garden to work He told them:
"I give you every seed bearing plant on the whole
face of the earth."
"Everything else you see I made it, this too I give to
the both of you."
The only rule was don't eat the forbidden fruit!
Now the craftiest of the wild animals that the Lord
made was the serpent
That told Eve lies
"If you eat that fruit it will just open your eyes"
Deceived by the serpent, Eve took a bite
In spite of what God said:
"If you eat that fruit you surely will die"
that was no lie
Wait, it gets worse
Then she gave her husband Adam a bite
That's when they realized God was right
They couldn't ignore their nakedness in front of the
Lord
God said; "What have you done?"
Adam said; "That women you put me here with
game me some"
Eve said "I was deceived"
So the Lord put a curse on all three

The serpent will crawl on its belly for the rest of his
life
While Adam will toil the earth to provide for his
wife
Eve was cursed with painful child birth,
not to mention a menstrual cycle
Man should not of been allowed to reach out it's
hand and take fruit from that tree
Here is the biggest mistake of man's life
laid out before thee....

Genesis 3:22-23

"The LORD God said, "Since man has become like one
of Us, knowing good and evil, he must not reach
out, take from the tree of life, eat, and live forever."
So the LORD God sent him away from the garden of
Eden to work the ground from which he was taken."

The ONE

Many people think Christmas is about santa, and
the many gifts he brings
But is really about the birth of our Savior
God blessed the precious night He was born
A world full of sin
Not one soul was able to claim that he's clean
BEHOLD a Mighty King
born in the most humblest of places
a manger, a place you would never think
would be the birth place of a man
that would change everything
Who would of knew that He would give His life for
you and for me that wondrous night
When the Star shined so bright
Leading the 3 wise to the young King
Oh what joy it brings to know that
we were given the chance to be with the Lord
By His one and only begotten son that He gave for
everyone

Luke 1:35

"The angel replied to her: "The Holy Spirit will
come upon you, and the power of the Most High
will overshadow you. Therefore, the holy One to be
born will be called the Son of God."

The Covenant

Rainbows are a promise
Made by God himself
In Genesis Chapter 9 verse 13
your can read it for yourself
They have so many colors
so every one can see
that the Lord loves us so dearly
He once destroyed earth's people with a flood
cause of the evil it contained
So he invented a rainbow
as a promise that he would never
destroy all living creatures again

If you're out one day
and you see a rainbow
remember why it was put in the sky...

Genesis 9:13

"I have placed My bow in the clouds, and it will be
a sign of the covenant
between Me and the earth."

More Than A Savior

Once you accept Him in your heart
Jesus is more than a Savior
there will be filth no more
He is the cleanser of the soul
These worldly duties are just our daily chores
He teaches us to look beyond the core,
to hold a grudge against our enemies no more
He was sent by our Heavenly Father
to teach God's real plan
No one else has stepped foot on this earth through a
virgin
not another soul in all the land
That's how you know there is none that compare to
Him,
the ONE without sin.
He taught us to Glorify our Heavenly Father
even though He was being slaughtered
What was man's reason when He died on that cross
He carried man's sins
He was treated like a man that committed the
worst things,
in between two thieves He died for all of mankind
It was through Him that we were granted access to
the heavenly gates
Before that dark was human fate

What We Do Unto Others

What we unto others affects the way we live
if you treat people badly
later on you they'll spit
if you feed a poor person
many blessing you will reap
Love is something that really exists
Most people don't stop to think
The things they do might come back quick

My motto is to treat all people nice
sometimes it costs me a substantial price
if your smart you'll know
the LORD is always watching
He saw when you opened the door for the old man
or when you helped the old lady bring her groceries
back from the store
Nobody has to know
Keep it between you and the LORD

Matthew 6:4

"...so that your giving may be in secret. And your
Father who sees in secret will reward you."

*How Deep Is Your Love? *

How far deep are the deepest depths of love?
Where does it end? How does it begin?
Is it something in the skin?
Or does it depends on what state of mind your in?
Maybe you have to really examine it
to know it's starting point and it's ending point
I think we don't really think about how deep love is
How the Lord is the only one that can measure
How deep your love goes
When judgment comes then you will know

Then you'll know exactly how many people were
truly loved by you and
how much you were really loved
If the love you thought was real
was what you thought it was
or were you living a lie
The ultimate love
is the one that comes from God
He has the purest love available for all mankind
something you can't buy cause it's divine...

God loves you all the time

Superficial

Stop being so superficial
With you everything is an issue
Like having something to eat
Or having a place to sleep
Don't you know if you ask God
you will never have a need?
And this is a guarantee
This is something I was told and
is something I believe
Though some people will not be able to see
How good God is to me
Some might say my life is a tragedy
But I say more like a mystery
People don't really understand me
That's okay
I don't need people to understand me to know that
I'm unique
There is no one else on earth like me
I don't like to think like everyone else
I enjoy being myself

Philippians 4:19

"And my God will supply all your needs according
to His riches in glory in Christ Jesus."

The One Who Wakes The Sun

God is the one that wakes the sun
He says:
It's time to wake up;
My children are waiting
for your warmth and light
Please be sure that you shine real bright
So that everyone could see
how My love for them gleams
that is why I put you in plain sight
Even though you shine so bright
there is still some children
that do not receive your light
I have a task for you
If you reach my children that your light can't see
I'll make sure to make you shine ever so brightly

And that is how the sun is woken up

Psalms 113:3

"From the rising of the sun to its setting the name
of the LORD is to be praised."

Another Day

It's a beautiful day
the first thing I want to say is
Thank you LORD for waking me up today!
Everywhere I go I see your art
It flows out from the world like a never-ending
spring
You are the creator of all things
To you I owe my very being
This body that I have is because of you
the soul that is in it
You put it there too!
I don't know what I would do without you
How wonderful it is to even think of you
it fills my heart with joy
that spills over my life
that once was full of strife

Lamentations 3:22

"Because of the LORD's faithful love we do not
perish, for His mercies never end."

The Story

I got a story to tell
God came to earth to save all of mankind
I don't understand why people are still blind
You want to know why He died?
He died for our sins
In order for Him to redeem
The pact between a Father and His children
See, the devil just came to slaughter
The Lord wants to invite you to a celebration
Of all nations
Everyone is allowed
and you don't have to pay to get in
You have to work by serving others
If you put yourself last then God will put you first
If you lived a poor life then God will make you rich
Spiritually that is...
So come to the Banquet and meet my friend
Jesus is His name
I am sure you will be amazed
Because the things that He does cannot be
explained
He is the son of the Most High

If I were you
My thoughts would be
"I want to meet the One that gave His life for me"
If you don't want to come that's okay
Just remember that the invitation still stands
As long as you are alive you still have a chance
Don't look back and take a glance
Because the devil has you in a trance
Behold as the future unfolds
Jesus is the story that will never finish being told
The soul is like the mist
You don't know of what it consists
You just know it exists
Give it what it needs
Salvation that only comes from the Lord

Psalms 19:4

"May the words of my mouth and the meditation of
my heart be acceptable to You, Lord, my rock and
my Redeemer."

My Ball Point Pen

My ball point pen
It gives my thoughts a voice
that will be recorded until
either burned, or torn
I spill my guts through my pen
A lot of hours I spend
Hoping somebody will comprehend
my mechanism
and how I tic
by the words that I write with my ball point pen
Sometimes the things that I write
I don't even understand
I just know that good thoughts shouldn't be wasted
they have to be written down

Only then can you judge
If what you wrote was a waste of time

And ink...

With my ballpoint pen I give Glory to my King!

Life Is Fragile Handle With Prayer

Life is fragile handle with prayer
The LORD is the only one who really cares
He's the one that knows when you feel like pulling
out your hair
He's the one that knows if your heart is in despair
He wants you to be careful out there
There's no telling what can happen if your not
aware
The devil's on the prowl
he's waiting to make you fall
he'll have up against the wall
With temptation all around.
If I was you I would call on the one that wears the
crown
With Him wisdom can be found
He'll make you sturdy on the ground
He'll be your foundation
With Him you can defeat temptation
He'll show you the revelations
We need to transport thoughts from one brain to
another
and that's how you spread the word
So the LORD can be heard
That's how you do your part if you really want to
serve

GOD you are to amazing for words!!!!
Most times you make me feel like I can handle
anything in the world.
Your the reason I'm strong
I don't know why it took me so long
Thank you LORD for the ability to speak
Without you I could not say a word
I want to know all you want me to say
I think that's my reason for living
My thoughts is to much for the average mind
I have what you call "Intricate Thinking"
You have to dissect my thoughts to really know
what I mean
To me sometimes this life seems like a dream
I just want to scream
Because my thoughts are flowing out like a stream
There's no explanation for the flow
it just knows it needs to be told
So right here my life will unfold
You will see and feel many things that were really
cold
People might say I was bold
to live this life that I live
and not let it drop me to my knees

But that's not a bad thing

All I know is that on my knees is where He humbles
me
I just think it is weak to not come up with a solution
to most people giving up is the resolution
Not me, not I!
This is why
The reason being, is that I was not designed to fail
only to prevail
And I know GOD wouldn't make no loser
That's the reason He chose me

Ephesians 6:18

"Pray at all times in the Spirit with every prayer
and request, and stay alert in this with all
perseverance and intercession for all the saints."

My Friend

Getting to know God is like getting to know one of
your friends
YOU have to spend time with Him
He loves it when we praise Him
He is God
He is worthy
He wants you to seek and ask
So you can find and receive His grace
We had a multi-million dollar debt
That God overpaid
Jesus is His name
"It is Finished" Jesus said
He absorbed all the pain
Our iniquities, on Him
God laid
All the shame
OH, But wait, It's not over yet
He came back to life again
HALLELUJAH!!!!!
The King Has risen
He conquered death
for our sake...
Don't you see
we are His Creation
He did all that so we could be with Him

Now, take the first step...

Get on your knees and pray to Him

He's been waiting for a long time

To hear from His precious child

Romans 10:9

"If you confess with your mouth, "Jesus is Lord,"
and believe in your heart that God raised Him
from the dead, you will be saved."

The Faithful One

You are faithful and true
I can only rely on you
Everyone else is human
they fail too
But God on the other hand
is too strong to ever fall
if you humble yourself
in due time
He will lift you tall
It's better to serve him
Than to sit around wondering
What's your purpose?
He is the reason that I am around
And not buried in the ground
Thank you Lord for finding me
when I didn't want to be found
I always tried to hide in the crowd
I'm such a fool
Thinking I can hide from You
You can see everything there is to see
So where can I flee?

Until Finally, I came out
And realized " I need to return to my Father's
house"
Out in the world I only felt Doubt
Never sure of what I felt
Like a loose wave out at sea
with no where to rest
Now I stand firm like a tree
thank you Lord for loving a person like me

Jeremiah 23:24

"Can a man hide himself in secret places where I
cannot see him?"--The LORD's declaration. "Do I not
fill the heavens and the earth?"--The LORD's
declaration."

Hope-filled Romantic

Daniel,
I love u more everyday
You're the man I always wanted
God blessed you with such a gorgeous face
You were cleverly designed
With me in mind
Every detail of your being is encrypted with the
evidence of God's perfection
As He took the time to think of every aspect of
your being
I get the privilege of enjoying your company
Since I have a Father that enjoys giving me the
desires of my heart
He knew you were for me from the start
That is why I must bless the Lord
After all you are exactly what I want
Today and forever you will always have my heart
I will cherish every moment with you
You are too good to be true
I love being with you
The God of all time said your mine....
Help me Lord to be the best wife
Someone Daniel can love for the rest of His life....
I Love You more than you can imagine
Thank You Lord for this handsome man of mine

The Ivy

The Love I have for you
Grows and grows and grows
Its like the ivy planted to decorate the wall
Right before we get to your block
I saw that little by little it grew
Clinging to the wall
Covering inch by inch
Next thing we knew
That once small ivy
The whole 100-foot wall had consumed
It reflected how
We were having so much fun
Just being with each other
That the days turned into months
And months turned into years
Look, we are still here!
Every time we turn that corner I look at the
wall of Ivy
It reminds me....
Of how much our love has continued to grow...
Thank God for Love
Because without Him there would be
No you or me
No ivy, no wall
There would be nothing at all....

His Will Be Done

God had a plan that was on His mind before time
began
He knew that He would create man
He also knew that we would fail to live as He had
planned
Deceived were we
By the evil serpent who was jealous of the Love
that God had for you and for me
In Genesis chapter 3 verse 15
God said that He would defeat the devil for all
eternity
2000 years went by and the promise came to pass
The Savior was born by the animals in a manger
Humbly He grew up until it was time to step up
In John 13 verse 18 you will see
Jesus had fulfilled the ancient Holy prophecy
He said " the one who eats my bread has raised
his heel against me"
The devil knew his time was near
When Jesus would pay the price for the sin of
Man
Because when Jesus died and rose from the dead
on the 3rd day

Death was dead
Now we would not be separated from the Creator of
all mankind
Access was granted
All we have to do now is believe
Next, we will be set free from the sin
That had a hold of you and I
God paid a colossal price for the ransom set for our
life
The check cleared the Third Day
Thank you Father

2 Timothy 1:19

*"He has saved us and called us with a holy calling,
not according to our works, but according to His
own purpose and grace, which was given to us in
Christ Jesus before time began."*

The HOLY ONE

He is The Holy ONE
He dwells in heaven, which is a much bigger space
He watches over his children
From His throne up above
You can get to him
Only if you go through His son

Isaiah 48:17

"This is what the LORD, your Redeemer, the Holy
One of Israel says: "I am Yahweh your God,
who teaches you for your benefit,
who leads you in the way you should go."

Remission Of Sins

Lord Jesus,
You are the on that died on the cross
for everyone
Your blood you shed on Calvary
Only Through your blood is there remission of sins
And forgiveness for all the bad things
You make everything new and grant us access to
your Father too!
You are the bridge that filled the gap
Between man and God
Through You
We retrieved what we lost many years back

Hebrews 9:22

"According to the law almost everything is purified
with blood, and without the shedding of blood there
is no forgiveness."

My Jesus

I trust you
I will not let doubt cross my mind
I will make my thoughts submit to your Holy Spirit
That lives inside my heart
Help me to defeat the devil when he comes at me
with lies
If it doesn't line up with your word I will pay no
mind
You're awesome all the time
I will not be afraid since I know that you're with
me
Thank you Jesus for the thoughts you put inside my
head
You even make them rhyme
Who would of knew in the past
That in the future I would make you mine
It just proves that the Lord can reach you at the
perfect time
Only then can you tell people of the things He has
done in your life
Words that might save someone's eternal soul
From the flames of hell
That can never be quenched
And the worms that will never die
In your body they will abide

If you don't choose The Messiah as your savior
Only then can you have His favor
Of this world I am not!
I was bought
With the Lambs precious blood
That was sacrificed for my life
I want to tell the world of the things you have done
for me
How you set me free!
Here in your house is where I want to be
I want to be your faithful servant
In spirit and in Truth
Help me My Jesus so I can be faithful to you

2 Corinthians 10:4-5

"...since the weapons of our warfare are not worldly, but are powerful through God for the demolition of strongholds. We demolish arguments and every high-minded thing that is raised up against the knowledge of God, taking every thought captive to obey Christ."

The Meaning Of Life

I think the meaning of life is to love and be loved
To change the world by changing yourself
To be a better person because you know what's
right
To help others even if they are still trying to fight
To not be afraid of being rejected
Because only You, Lord love unconditionally
I think the Lord is the only one who really
understands me
Worldly people don't know who Love really is
So I can't sit here and explain
If you have not gotten to that point yet
I think the meaning of life is being content with
yourself as well as with your circumstances
Since no matter what there are always problems
You don't have to agree with what I say
I know everyone has their own perspective
It's not unexpected
I think the meaning of life is to treat mean people
nice
To show them that you are not like them
No matter how hard they try to get you to give in
People ask me: Why am I so nice?
Because God said!!!!
He is the Way the Truth and the Life

Aware

I don't know if you are aware
I want to let you know that the Lord always cares
Sometimes He takes a long time to answer a prayer
But I assure you that
God's time is the best time
He's got you in mind
All the time
Your name He gave you before time began
He knit us, like quilts in the wombs of our mothers
His love for you He proved
When His arms He spread wide
And was nailed to the cross of Calvary

Psalms 139:13

"For it was You who created my inward parts; You
knit me together in my mother's womb."

What Flows Inside Me

I can't explain the living waters that come from
inside me
It once was filled with strange and evil things
Now I got living springs
You want to know what makes me feel like this?
JESUS
He took up all of humanity's sin upon Him
I don't know anybody else that gave up all their
wealth
For a girl like me that never appreciated a thing
Now I realize that without Him I'm nothing
To start you must invite Him in your heart
Then you must look for a church that you feel at
home in
The next step is to start serving Him
There your talents will be revealed
He will show you things the devil tried to conceal
So you wouldn't have dreams, goals
or expectations
My poetry for me is a revelation of things I thought
I could never be
That is why here you will see
what flows inside of me
Thank you Jesus for what you did for my Family
as well as for loving a rebellious girl like me!!!!

Answered Prayer

The little boy I prayed for is on his ways
By the grace of God everything will be okay
Yahweh
My prayers I put before you I know I can rely on
you
You've answered them and I want to tell the world
about what you do
I love to serve you
I want You to be happy with my service to You
To put a smile on your face is what I want to do
I chose life
If I don't I will not get to be with you

Lord please help us
In the middle of our trials, tribulations and
temptations
Help us to focus
The Lord is sovereign and can't be moved from His
throne!!!

My Purpose

He has a purpose for my life
Before the foundation of the world
He knew me
In my mother's womb You formed me
All through my life you have been with me
I sometimes fail
When I do I get mad at myself
So I pray for you to make my path straight
That you may please open up the window of
opportunity
That can help me flee from temptation
Keep me on the narrow path
I know You are there because you reveal Yourself
to me
Help me to always remember the day I saw you
As clear as a star in the sky on the clearest day

When you told me you loved me...

Stay Focused

To keep your dreams alive you have to stay focused
Before I felt sorrow
Now I look forward to a new tomorrow
My Goal is to become a successful writer
I just keep thinking that one day I'll be gone
If I write it will keep my memory strong
I will leave something behind
That expresses how I felt inside
My work
That will stay on this earth

Unlike my soul that will have a rebirth
To a place better than earth

I have too much inside to keep to myself
I will give my thoughts to the paper
It will receive it
So people can perceive it
Thank you Lord for everything you have given to
me
Without you I don't know where I would be

Pastora Rosa

Ever since I walked through those doors
You have treated me so kindly
You have done a lot for me
I love that we have so much in common
You're my Pastor, my sister in Christ, & you're also
my family
You make serving God fun and elegant
You do everything with excellence
God is so wise
He always puts the right people in our lives
You've been a huge blessing to my family and I
Your words and experience have brought me
comfort
When I faced my biggest life obstacles
You have always been a great example
You really mean a lot to me
We've crossed valleys, rivers and storms together
Through it all I've realized you've encouraged me
through
I'm very thankful for you
I pray that God blesses you and your beautiful
family
Your marriage, your children, your job, your home,
and all that pertains to you

I also pray that God continues to use you to lift
others up
You have encouraged me to never give up
In the trenches I will be with you and with our
congregation
Till I die
Or the Lord comes back to pick us up
Thank you for being who you are
A beautiful woman from Chihuahua
That loves the Lord and His church
That helps to Pastor His flock!!!
I love you!!!

Jeremiah 3:15

"I will give you shepherds who are loyal to Me, and
they will shepherd you with knowledge and skill."

Pastor Eddie

You are a blessing
Chosen by God with unction
To preach His word with conviction
So that we may live right before our Father
You live His word and fear the Lord
You give us the example: to only look to the Lord
and not the defects of those that surround us
I think Jehovah is very proud of you and all the
hard work you have put into His Vineyard
Furthermore I think that the Lord is fascinated by
the way you direct worship
You are blessed with such a beautiful family
Our family's desire is that the Lord releases the
entire blessings that for you He has in store
So that along with your family they can be enjoyed
We share in your joy
The word of God teaches us that we should obey our
Pastors
Including submitting to their authority
For me that is not a problem
Since I understand that you will have to give an
account to Him
For all the souls that have walked through those
doors

May the Lord bless you with a double portion of
His mercies, blessings, grace and love

Continue to bring forth more souls to the kingdom
of God
Since you were the instrument God used to reunite
me back with Him
Thank you Pastor Eddie
All the glory is for our Heavenly Father

Isaiah 52:7

"How beautiful on the mountains are the feet of the
herald, who proclaims peace, who brings news of
good things, who proclaims salvation, who says to
Zion, "Your God reigns!"

Love

Love is who you are
Love is what you give
You are eternal
Your Greatness is never-ending
As well as your knowledge
That lays bare for you to see
Just like death
That could not hold you
To get your children back

1 John 4:8

"The one who does not love does not know God,
because God is love."

Creative Father

The Lord has a purpose for everything in life
All the poems that I write
Even for the things that happened in my life
God is the most creative being
He comes up with all sorts of ideas to get people to
know that He is King
He wants you to be with Him
Trust Him today
Let go of your past
He will make you new
That way you can pursue all your dreams and your
goals
He knows everything that has gone on in your
heart
From the very start ever since you were born
He even knows all the hairs you have grown
Don't wait any longer and call on your Heavenly
Father...

2 Corinthians 5:17

"Therefore, if anyone is in Christ, he is a new
creation; old things have passed away, and look,
new things have come."

The Never-ending Spring

The Love I have for you just cannot be described
I can only compare it to the things I see in life
It comes from within and cannot be contained
It spills over everything that gets in its way
The source never runs dry
There is a surplus at hand
Since my love is always in demand
Everyone wants a piece of me
I don't understand
The Lord said to walk in love
That is the task at hand
You're my peace
The one that holds my hand
Through all my strife
You made me love life again!

The Life Jacket

The Lord threw this drowning world a life jacket
Some choose to drown
While others want to live
They choose to receive the gift
To uplift them from death and torment
Which is the consequence of sin
I don't want to lust for nothing in this world
It only brings corruption and destruction
The Lord is my desire
Of Him I will inquire

Today I ask do you want to drown or do you want
to live?
If your answer is yes
Then
Put on your life jacket and start living for Him!

2 Peter 3:9

"The Lord does not delay His promise, as some
understand delay, but is patient with you, not
wanting any to perish but all to come to
repentance."

Glisten

This for all you girls that just don't listen
You don't need a man to make you feel like you
glisten
All you need is Jesus
He is the gentleman that is knocking at your door
Please invite Him in
Dine with Him
See what He has in store
He has a better future than the one you have in
mind
He knows everything from Start to Finish
Please put your trust and hope
In the only one that can save your soul
And renew your mind with His word that can
change your life

Psalms 118:8

"It is better to take refuge in the LORD than to
trust in man."

Healing Love

His love heals me
Jesus understands me
He knows exactly what bothers me
I put Him in charge to guide my life
To help me to consistently live in His light
Darkness is not what He wants for me
He shed His blood to set us free
In bondage we no longer have to be
Yet sometimes I backslide from His presence
Please Father forgive me...

Romans 8:20-21

"For the creation was subjected to futility—not willingly, but because of Him who subjected it—in the hope that the creation itself will also be set free from the bondage of corruption into the glorious freedom of God's children."

Lord,

Great is you're your mercy towards me
You're my father that disciplines, and directs me
Even though I fall you lift me up
Thank you for your never-ending love that breaks
me
I'm not worthy
Yet you call me daughter
Please Lord; help me to be stronger and to be
a good example
For my sons and my daughters
I know they watch everything I do
Your Word spoke to my heart
You told me to never forget that you are Love
Thank you for reminding me
Sometimes I get tired and my mind gets lost
Where it shouldn't be
Renew my strength and use me
So that You is what people see!!!
I know that You are with me
Sometimes I forget and choose not to obey
Father please forgive me
I do love you

Help me to constantly keep walking
In Spirit and in Truth
Keeping in mind your kingdom
Which is at hand
Put your words in my mouth so I can preach to all
I can
Guide me and teach me
That way I can live worthy of your calling
My loyalty I want to give You
Only to You
My Prince of Peace and Wonderful Counselor
My Everlasting Father

Isaiah 9:6

"For a child will be born for us, a son will be given
to us, and the government will be on His shoulders.
He will be named Wonderful Counselor, Mighty
God, Eternal Father, Prince of Peace. "

The enemy

The devil is everywhere
You can defeat Him with
God's word, fasting and prayer
he will promise you fame and lots of wealth
he is very stealth
he also hides very well
We must open up our spiritual eyes to see the evil
that he is plotting
Grab your shield of faith
Extinguishing
The flaming arrows of the devil
Put on your helmet of salvation
Protecting your mind from all the temptation that
you're facing
Then grab your double-edged sword
It is God's Word
That exposes all the devil's work
That's the only thing that hits him where it hurts
Keep your armor on
Never get complacent

The devils is lame
Jesus came and suffered a lot of pain
For you and for me
Through His sacrifice on the cross He wants to set
us free
From the trap of our enemy
that hates your guts and hopes to see you in hell
Where he will torture you beyond compare
Jesus came so that would not be your end
In Him you have a promise of a new life
Please allow Him in

1 John 3:8

"The one who commits sin is of the devil, for the
devil has sinned from the beginning. The Son of God
was revealed for this purpose: to destroy the devil's
works."

U Turn

God allows U turns
If your life is in shambles and you want it to
change
Make a u turn and turn around from the life you
live
Then start a new life with the King of kings
Let Him clean you of your sin
You must also read your Bible

His word says we all fell short of His glory
This is His love story
Every time I read it with Him I fall more in love
So what do you say?
Do you want to make a U turn today?

Romans 3:23

"For all have sinned and fall short of the glory of
God."

Amazing

Under the definition of Amazing you will find God
He is the definition of that word
He can do any and all things
So can you through Him that strengthens you
He loves us all even though we don't all love Him
He never stops trying
Even though at times we offend Him
When we turn our backs on Him
You want to know why?
Its because He wants to be our father
He showed us His love at all cost
His only Son He did not deny due to His Love
I can't thank Him enough

Philippians 4:13

"I am able to do all things through Him who
strengthens me."

Hell

Hell is real
Just like the pain you feel
It is where you will certainly go if here on earth
You don't choose the Lord
Remember that the Lord will not force you to love
Him
He cries when you deny Him
Access to your heart
He wants to help you get rid of all the things that
have been tearing you apart
He knows your pain, joy and sorrow
He hopes you won't wait until tomorrow
Who knows if it will come?
You can't win salvation
It's a gift from the Heavenly Father who sent His
only Son
Who died on a cross
That's where He shed His blood

He's coming back for His church that is wearing
white and is wrinkle free
Today Let the Lord iron our your wrinkles
With His saving power
He will clean you of all your filthy sin
Without Him you will never be clean
Give your life to Him and He will take care of
everything
Whatever it is
He will take care of it
Turning wretched to saved
It is His specialty
Especially since He is the Lord of lords and King of
kings!!!!
Mighty is HE!!!

Matthew 13:41-42

"The Son of Man will send out His angels, and they
will gather from His kingdom everything that
causes sin and those guilty of lawlessness. They will
throw them into the blazing furnace where there
will be weeping and gnashing of teeth."

Lord,

My heart is to beat up to take another blow
It has to recover slowly
It is something only You can console
You know exactly what it takes to turn my sorrow
into joy
I need your perfect comfort
The peace that only you can give
Every time I face a trial
You know exactly what to do
You said " Do not let your heart be troubled, you
believe in God, believe also in me "
In this life you will have tribulations
Take heart I have overcome the world"
You are the Big Bang
There is no one that can stand a chance
To go against your Wisdom, Knowledge and Power
You are my strong tower

Please Lord help me recover from yet another blow
to my heart and soul
Only with your help can I get through this storm of
emotions
Filled with "what if's"

Light Of My Life

Jesus Christ
The light of my life
Your love I just can't comprehend
How the earth in space you suspend
The stars you know them all by name
The water on this earth fills but the palm of your
hand
The mountains are but dust to You
Your are so worthy of my praise
I delight in serving You
All of my days
I think about you everyday
Every wonder that I see
You put it in its place just for me
Thanks to Your amazing grace
The knowledge on this earth are just words to You
There is no limit to Your knowledge
Who can stand up to You?
I know no one who can fill Your shoes
A loving father
The best kind of friend
Who will never leave you but be with you till the
end

Parable Of The Great Banquet

There was a King that prepared a great
banquet
For all His family and friends
Since His Son was getting married
But most were too busy to attend
The King tried again
His servants He sent to tell the invited guests
that the best food in all the land
was prepared and was ready for them to
dine with Him and His Son
Sadly the servants were tortured and murdered
for bugging them because work and other things
were much more important
The King then sent His army to get rid of all of
them for their ungratefulness
Since He had went out of His way for them
Then He sent more servants to gather all the
people they could find
The ones that He invited first did not deserve
to come
People good and bad filled the banquet hall
The king came in to see who was present to
dine with Him and His Son
He noticed one not wearing wedding attire

The king then asked him
"How did you get in?"
"Why don't you have on your wedding clothes?"
So the King summoned His servants to tie him up
from his hands and his feet
He was thrown out into the darkest darkness
This too can be you
If you refuse God's invitation to be wed to His Son
Please understand that Jesus is the groom and His
church is His bride
The Lord is courting you today
Please let go of your pride
There is no one else that will love as much as He
So much so that He died for thee and me
Jesus's blood will wash you of your filthiness
That way He can look at your loveliness
Though our sin is as red as crimson
He can make us white as snow
Lets put on our wedding clothes and be wed to the
King of Kings & Lord of lords
Your soul desires nothing more!

Matthew 22:13

"Then the king said to the servants, 'Bind him hand
and foot, and throw him into the outer darkness; in
that place there will be weeping and gnashing of
teeth."

Mighty To Save

You are mighty to save
So mighty that:
I was in your thoughts
Before time began
Oh what a great Lord we have
His death was not in vain
I realize that it was for me that He was slain
My sins were a crimson stain
But Behold the Lamb of God took all our sins away
He nailed them to the cross
He put the devil and his minions to shame
A spectacle of them He made
In your face satan!!!
Jesus Saves!!!!
He was not distracted by any of his tactics
Glory to the Father He gave
When He rose from the grave on the third day
Then He revealed Himself to those He loved and
died to save
We too have access to that gift
You must realize that you are a sinner that wants
and needs to be saved
Today can be that day

The Mind Of Christ

To have the mind of Christ you have to read His
word
Those were His
"Basic Instructions Before Leaving Earth"
It teaches us how to act, react, respond, expect,
reject
Please don't neglect it
It is the advise of a Father
To His many sons and daughters
If People do not accept Him
They cannot be called His children
From what I know
Children like to please their father
When you accept Him He'll give you His Holy
Spirit
With His guidance is the only way you will succeed
On the other hand if you're walking in the flesh
Then you will only think about fleshly desires
Including all the things you can acquire
Their treasure is here on earth and not in heaven
Where the moth will eat it and it will rot
Eternity is not on their mind
Only Money, pleasure, & power
The devil has their eyes covered
This is why we need the Mind of Christ
So that the devil doesn't lead us away from the
Father

Dear Lord,

Blessed be your name
You are the only True God
Like you there is no other
My life is nothing without you
Please help me to think like You
Apparently my heart deceives me
I can now see it clearly
Invade my mind
Please take over
Because I have committed treason
I fail you and at times neglect you
Forgive and Help ME
I am under attack
Yet I do nothing about it
WHY!!!
Holy Spirit Help me
I've saddened you and Hurt you
I'm so sorry...
I really need your assistance
Renew my mind today
By your limitless power
Help me to change my habits that do not please you
That also hinders my walk with you

Lord, You are mighty to save
I need You to take control of my life
Including my actions
That can result in me living my life according to
Your Holy Word
I really want to live for you and dedicate my
talents to you
I want to give you all the glory and honor that you
deserve
Be my one and only
Only You really know me
Remove any deceit from me
My petition is for you to help me line up my life to
your will
Please break the chains that unknowingly I may
have put on myself
At your feet I leave this for you

Ephesians 4:30-31

"And don't grieve God's Holy Spirit. You were
sealed by Him for the day of redemption. Get rid
of all bitterness, rage and anger, brawling and
slander, along with every form of malice."

"My Grace Is Sufficient"

Those are Jesus's words to you and me
Depending on Him in all you do
Your weakest moment can be your best moment
It is there that He can be strong for you
Overcoming obstacles that without Him you could
never do
We don't deserve His grace and favor
But because He loves you and I so much
He still decided to give it to you and I
On the cross He displayed His love for all to see
Now will you let Him be?
Your savior, your friend, the one that will be with
you till the end?
Will you let Him be your grace, your strength, and
your provider?
My answer is YES!
To things that I don't deserve
To grace that saves
To love that never fades
To my name written in the Lamb's Book of Life
To trusting Him even when things don't look so
great

The crazy thing about it is that there is nothing
I could of done to earn it
I simply had to choose it
I had to accept the gift Christ gave
When He gave His life for me

I ask you today
Will the grace that He gave have gone in vain?
Or are you going to accept God's undeserved
kindness?
Then give Him glory and praise?

2 Corinthians 12:19

"But He said to me, "My grace is sufficient for you,
for power is perfected in weakness." Therefore, I
will most gladly boast all the more about my
weaknesses, so that Christ's power may reside in
me."

Master Creator

We are not all God's Children
But we are all His crown creation
To become a child of God you must receive Him
Then in Christ we become a new creation
All the old things pass away
After that we must realize that we should live our
lives with certain limitations

We are all God's manufacture product
Created by the Master Artisan Himself which
means we are real expensive
Since it took Him a lot of time and dedication
To think up all the details of our being
And it was really pricey for Him when our very
lives He sought then bought

Jesus Is Lord

Jesus is Lord and no one can top Him
The most High God
Yahweh Yireh, Yahweh Nissi, & Yahweh Rafah
He promises to take care of all your needs
Believe Him
Trust Him with your heart
He will guard it with His life
Jesus Christ died on a wooden cross to prove you
were worth every drop
of blood that He shed
He wouldn't of had it any other way
He wants to be discovered by you as you go
throughout your day
Look for His invisible Hand
That moves throughout the whole land
With only one stroke of His hand
The ocean is but a puddle to Him
The whole earth but a grain of sand in the Masters
Hand
So to all the inhabitants of the Land
Recognize that He is God and your man on that
grain of sand
And TODAY salvation is at hand!

For The Youth

Please take a second look
You'll see a girl with a lot of defects
One that use to be a crook and a con artist
Caught up in a life of crime
There was even a point in time when I thought
"I'm a lost cause"
Who cares anyways?
I couldn't even get my dad to stick around
To take care of me
My Mom was never proud of me
I felt sorry for myself for several years
Till 2004 when I faced the biggest tragedy
So I thought....
My children's father Rene was murdered right
in front of my children, his brother and I
There was nothing I could have done to change
the outcome
Everything I had said and done had caught up
to me
Even then the Lord had mercy on me
How could He?
I backslid and forgot about everything He
promised me
I had sat a man on the throne of my heart that
belonged to God

I was a young girl in love thinking I had
everything lined up
Not until the smoke settled did I realize how bad
I had messed up
Now I had two mouths to feed
And broken pieces all around me
I then gathered up the courage to pick up my Bible
I was afraid of what He would say to me
Psalm 18 verses 16 through 19
His word confirmed what I knew in my heart
was true
"He reached down from heaven and took a hold of
me
He rescued me from my powerful enemy
And those that hated me, for they were too strong
for me
They confronted me in the day of distress
But the Lord was there for me
He brought me out to a wide-open place
He rescued me because He delighted in me"
I knelt and I cried due to all the hurt I held inside
I smoked all day to numb the pain
Little by little the Lord conquered me with His love
Later on I met Daniel
On a day I didn't want to get out of bed
The Lord used his mom Reyna to bring me back to
His courts of Prayer and Praise

Then the Lord said:
In Isaiah 54 verse 4 through 8
"Do not be afraid for you will not be put to shame
Don't be humiliated, you will not be disgraced.
For you will forget the shame of your youth
And you will no longer remember the disgrace of
your widowhood
For your husband is your maker, His name is
Yahweh
The Holy One of Israel
Your redeemer
The God of all the earth
For He has called you like a wife deserted and
wounded in spirit
The wife of one's youth
when she is rejected
I deserted you but a moment
But I will take you back with great compassion
In a surge of anger I hid my face from you
For a moment
But I will have compassion on you with everlasting
love
Says the Lord your Redeemer."
When I got to His house I was tired and thirsty
I had crossed a desert and was left without strength
Not to mention I was pregnant
As Pastor Eddie preached
My deepest darkest secrets were laid bare right

before me
The Father I had avoided all these years let me
know He was here
I remember Pastor Eddie telling me:
"Angie, you need to get right with the Lord, your
living in fornication and you know that in God's
eyes that isn't right"
My heart sank!
"If you want to get right with the Lord, I will help
you do just that"
He married us on March 14, 2009
I was pregnant during the whole ordeal
It was such a relief
Our daughter was born a month later
To our disbelief
When she was 20 months old
What I now call an even bigger tragedy
Occurred on January 14, 2011
She had gotten ran over by my neighbor
Trust me I know, it is something hard to believe
The blow was too big, even for me
She passed away on the 15th
All I could do was to forgive
It's what Jesus had taught me
My flesh didn't want to but my spirit knew it was
the right thing to do
When we do what God has asked us to do
He quickly rushes in

With your obedience you are telling Him that
you trust in Him
Regardless if what you are facing is really big
The Lord glorified Himself and about ten
thousand dollars came in
From everyone that wanted to help
See, I don't have to understand His will
Instead He wanted me to rest in His love while He
comforted my broken heart
I don't even know how I got out of that one
My marriage survived the blow
It's a miracle! Is all I know!
The hardest part was forgiving myself
*****

Before long the Lord sent Sofia to help ease the Pain
Daniel Jr. Soon followed
God knows what to do at the turn of every page
But wait it doesn't end there
Another baby was on his way
I know what your thinking
Another Baby?
This time it did not end so great
When I went to the hospital to have my little
bundle of Love
To my dismay
I saw an alarming look on the nurse's face
"What, what do you mean you cant find the heart
beat?"

Now this devastating blow really took a toll on me
I gave birth to a stillborn son named David on
May 27th 2014
That really hurt!!!
The only baby I got to name was not going home
with me
How could I face another day?
Some would say
By the mighty hand of the Lord
That's the only way!
I came home to a house full of things that people
had showered me with
But no baby!
I cried and cried and cried
So I gave all the things away
Turns out my baby's stuff blessed a family that had
nothing to welcome their baby with
The Lord comforted me with the hugs and love of
those around me
So much so that almost exactly a year later the
Lord sent us a son named Samuel on June 16, 2015
That was it for me
I had everything a girl could want
Beautiful children
Lalo, Sonia, Sofia, Junior, Samuel and my loving
Husband
Most importantly I had God's love that surrounded
me

During my whole teen and adult life I had
always clashed with my Mom
When I restarted walking with the Lord I knew I
had to conquer her with Love
It was like a boxing match
Every time she hit me with rejection I would swing
back with love and affection
But don't get me wrong
There were times I was down for the count
Like when she told me that I didn't miss my
daughter Sarah
Good thing I had my armor on
I replied, "Mom, the word of God says that no one
can truly know your joy or your sorrow…. Just
because I didn't bring you the cup of tears that I
cried doesn't mean I'm not hurting inside!
I'm the one trying to cheer you up when my heart
is broken."
The referee almost got to 10 before I got back up
See in this life you must use the word of God as your
sword to attack against all the negative darts
thrown at you
12th and final round
My Mom and I hashed everything out that caused
division between us
She accepted the Lord in my house
When Pastor Eddie ordained the renewing of her
vows

Victory for team Jesus!!!!!
The devil got knocked out
A year later she got really sick, went to the hospital
and never made it out
May 12th 2016 was the day she went to be with Lord
My Mom couldn't of made me more proud
Even though we had our ups and downs
The girl you see today is a result of God and the
Mom that He choose for me
She taught me dignity, humility, and respect
I'm thankful to the Lord that I was able to handle
my Mom's attitude the way He told me
That resulted in us being at peace with each other
before she left to be with Him
The Lord doesn't stop surprising me yet!
I tell you today if your broken and depressed
You're in the right place
Church, that is!
Where healing can take place
Take it from me, I've been dealt some pretty hard
blows
But as you can see the Lord is with you in every
obstacles life throws
His word says in
Isaiah 41 verse 10 "Do not fear for I am with you
Do not be afraid for I am your God and I will
strengthen you
I will help you!

*I will hold on to you with my righteous
right hand"
Not only that in Isaiah 43 verse 2
He says to you and I:
"I will be with you when you pass through the
waters and when you pass through the rivers
they will not overwhelm you
You will not be scorched when you pass through
the fires
The flame will not burn you"
Be of good courage and let the joy of the Lord
fill you with hope as you cope
With everyday life
He will never leave you or forsake you is His
faithful promise
Isaiah 44 verse 22 says:
"I have swept away your transgression like a
cloud and your sins like a mist
Return to me
For I have redeemed you"
His own life He laid to pay the debt for you simply
because He loves you*

He has turned my mourning into dancing
And on this mountaintop I'm announcing
That God is good no matter what you're facing

Accept the Lord today
Don't wait till it's too late
God bless you!

Acts 4:12

"There is salvation in no one else, for there is no other name under heaven given to people, and we must be saved by it."

Master Plan

I'm an Aztec queen
Who loves to read
I also love to write
Most of all I love serving God
He's so fun
He gives me all I need
He even supplies my wants
All He asks for in return is my heart
He gave all there was to give
For you and for me!
I love Him because He first loved me
I'm a girl that knows the master plan
God thought it up before time began
It started with the Word
"Let there be light" were the first words
Heard by nothing
Yet understood by everything
That spoke everything into existence
Every single thing we see
Lord, was first your idea
Even all the flowers are all unique
There is none like the other
This is another way that you show us there is but
one Father
Man is not God

If he were, there would be no need for hospitals
or doctors
There were be no need for healing
The God I know will never die
Why do we need funeral homes?
It's obvious that Yahweh is the one that gives life
I know we are not gods because only He could give
and ant a heart that is microscopic
With that being said
For all of you that think you're gods
STOP IT!!!
If we were God, why is it that we are the ones that
will have to give Him an account of our lives?
HIS WORD SAYS:
"Now brace yourself like a man. I will question
you, and you will answer Me."
Proving my point that if were God, wouldn't it be
the other way around?
I've never known a cloud that asked a man
"Is it okay if I come out?"
Also I have never known of a man that gave the
boundaries to the sea and land
I do know of the Heavenly Father that gave His
only begotten Son resulting in unity with Him
No man can ever love as much as God loved man
In conclusion even before time began
God was still God and man was just a part in His
Master plan....

The Test

God test our Love, obedience, loyalty, humility
and faith
He only tests us so we can prosper
And so we can live life abundantly
If people think that walking with the Lord is easy
They couldn't be more wrong!
Living the will of God should bring us true
satisfaction
He test us like gold to examine the quality and
exactitude of our attitude
That means that we will face many different types
of trials and tribulations
So that He can see what our reaction will be
His desire for us to pass and not fail
Only with His divine strength can we truly prevail
While satan temps us to make us fall and sin
God only test us to see if all of our dependence is
only on Him

Jeremiah 17 :10

"I, Yahweh, examine the mind,
I test the heart to give to each according to his way,
according to what his actions deserve."

Service Unto The Lord

Question?
Why do you serve the Lord?
It is so you can be seen by others?
Or is it that you appreciate that for you He left His
throne?
Is it because of what He can give you and the many
benefits that come with serving Him?
Or is it because you understand that He gave till
there was nothing left to give?
When He was on earth Jesus served and set the
ultimate example, there is no excuse!
If the Lord of lords and the King of kings can get on
His knees and wash the feet of His disciples
Are we too good to serve to that same extent?
Not worrying about ourselves but putting the needs
of others first
Showing our loved ones that we truly know the
Lord
The Word of God says that is the only way they will
know
We must walk in love
Visit the prisoners, go to the hospitals, feed
the poor
Setting a good example by not being prideful
Instead being humble before all

Jackie

There is so much to say about a person as great as
you...
First, I love the way you praise God and you made
me want to praise God again too!
God has used you in so many ways
To bless me and at times to lead the way
It shows that you allow the Lord to work through
you
I have felt His presence when you pray for me
And as you have walked in love always
With my Family and I
You're an amazing teacher
Your dedication to your ministry
Is unbelievable
You lead us into worship with such grace
I know for a fact that as you do, you put a big smile
on our Father's face
I'm so blessed to call you my sister in Christ and my
best friend
We clicked right from the start
Your so thoughtful and super fun to be around
Your passions to serve God helps to me stand firm
when my legs are giving out

I love all your creative ideas that you bring to
God's kingdom
It is a visible fruit of your personal walk with
our Lord
Your beautiful daughters all reflect you
I'm sure that your husband is very proud to be
with you
I join you in prayer
For Yahweh to grant your number 1 Petition
That one-day we will all see your husband serve
alongside of you
By faith I will wait with you for mine too!
Jackie, I'm very proud of you
I'm so blessed to know you and I want to let you
know that all those times you've showed up to lift
me up
Are all treasured deep inside my heart
I will always keep thanking God for you
May our Father richly bless you in all you do!!!

Proverbs 14:24

"A man with many friends may be harmed,
but there is a friend who stays closer than a
brother."

Father

Sorry for continually failing you
And not caring about the things you planned for
me to do
Forgive me for ignoring and at times
misrepresenting you
I've put Daniel before you
That's what I said I would not do
Why am I forgetting how far you have brought me
through?
Oh spirit of mine'
Listen to your Father this time
Holy Spirit
I have hurt you and made a mess along the way
I know I have not done your will and have allowed
myself to go astray
I've turned back to my old ways
PLEASE don't let me stay that way!!!
Remind me of your truth and please don't give up
on me
Guide me, lead me and revive me!!!
I need you desperately
I'm the deer panting for water
So stupid of me that I passed up the source
Help me to focus!

I've been distracted by the devils tactics
Because I'm selfishly focusing on myself instead
of everyone else

That ends today!
Father I pray that you help me in every way
I have no one else
Where else would I go?
Rip out all that saddens, hurts and upsets you
You deserve for me to be faithful to you
Redirect my thoughts back to your ways
For good this time
Since it was your goodness that led me to
repentance
Please forgive me...

John 14:26

"But the Counselor, the Holy Spirit--the Father will
send Him in My name--will teach you all things
and remind you of everything I have told you."

For My Children

Please show my children that you're their Savior,
their Redeemer, and their best friend
The only one that will stick around till the end
My babies, you are special in my eyes and in the
Lord's eyes
No matter who rejects you
Our Heavenly Father will always accept you
When I die I pray that you don't backslide
Stay on the Road that leads to Eternal Life
It won't be easy sometimes
Trust me your momma knows
Just remember that God is always in control
If you fail, its okay, when you do just get back up
Dust yourself off, start making good choices again
& Always read your Bible
Let the Holy Spirit Lead the way!

Deuteronomy 11:18-19

"Imprint these words of mine on your hearts and
minds, bind them as a sign on your hands, and let
them be a symbol on your foreheads.
Teach them to your children, talking about them
when you sit in your house and when you walk
along the road, when you lie down and when you
get up."

I Need You

I need you Lord like the mountains need the
snow so the creeks can overflow
I need you like the stars need the dark night so
they can shine real bright
I need you like an infant that is helpless
That needs someone to take care of him
I need you like the flowers need the sun
That's shines up above and gives what they need so
they can grow
I need you like trees need their roots
since without them they can give no fruit
I need you like the fish need the sea
Or else where would they swim?
I need you like my body needs my spirit
It's what encapsulates me
I am your vessel
I need you in my heart
so you can clean all that is evil within
I need you like a guitar needs its strings
because then it would only be a wooden thing
I need you like the birds need the sky
Or else where would they fly?
Finally I need you like a little girl needs her father
Only He can take care of her like no other
I need you till the day I die
Especially since you're the only reason I'm alive

139

Society Today

Today's society only lives for wealth
As thought they are exempt from death
They don't want to realize that they will have to
face Judgment
If their name is not written in the Lamb's Book of
Life
Nothing good awaits them
After this life
This is not meant to scare you but to make you
aware
I don't know if they know that their spirit lives
forever
You'll either end up in the Lake of Lava or you will
go to heaven
There are only two paths
Please don't be deceived
The devil's job is to keep us distracted
People don't even see!
God wanted to save us from this place called hell
No one was worthy
He had to come and sacrifice Himself
Only He was rich enough to pay the price
I pray that you put your trust in Him today
Let His word guide your life

Jesus

Jesus, you make me whole
You complete my very soul
Without you I would be out of control
With you I feel stable and able
To conquer my dreams and my fears
With you I feel sure and secure
You are my world
Thank you Lord for making me more precious than
a ruby, a diamond or a pearl

Colossians 2:9-10

"For the entire fullness of God's nature dwells bodily
in Christ, and you have been filled by Him, who is
the head over every ruler and authority."

The Truth

I put my trust in the King of Kings
The Lord of Lords
No one else can save you
Not Buddha or Gandhi
This yoga thing about your third eye is simply
blinding
Making people think that on their own they are
surviving
I don't know if you this, but you didn't make
yourself
You are a created being
Jesus is the owner of all truth and knowledge
No one else rose from the dead not even Mohamed
For us He conquered death
Ever since Adam and Eve we are all born into sin
Despite their downfall God already had a plan
He is not a human being
He always has the upper hand
I don't know if you understand that the devil hates
you
He wants to keep you separated from your creator
Why do you think you always find something to do
when someone invites you to go to church or to
read His word?
Trust me I've been there
A lot of people go around this life so unaware

Of the spiritual battle that happens in the air
Women chasing after men that can't even save
themselves
Men and women just being with each other for
sexual pleasure
Exploiting what God meant for the marriage bed
This society has tried to do away with fidelity and
morality
It's not like God just doesn't want you to have fun
He just wants you to save yourself for the right one

Ephesians 3:10-13

"Finally, be strengthened by the Lord and by His
vast strength. Put on the full armor of God so that
you can stand against the tactics of the Devil. For
our battle is not against flesh and blood, but against
the rulers, against the authorities, against the world
powers of this darkness, against the spiritual forces
of evil in the heavens. This is why you must take up
the full armor of God, so that you may be able to
resist in the evil day, and having prepared
everything, to take your stand."

Getting Through

I thank you my Lord Jesus for helping me get
through all the tough times in my life
Only you know just what to do
I also thank you for the good times too
You have always been there for me and for my
family
That's why again I want to thank you for the
things you have help me through
You have molded me with time and refined me to
be like you
People have let me down before
That helped me to realize that only You never will
Thank you Lord Jesus for the life you have renewed

Isaiah 40:31

"Youths may faint and grow weary,
and young men stumble and fall, but those who
trust in the LORD will renew their strength;
they will soar on wings like eagles;
they will run and not grow weary;
they will walk and not faint."

LOVE over HATE

Today we must choose *love* over hate
It is time
Let's not procrastinate
I'm the type of girl who will be quick to say
"Hey girl, you look great!!"
We are all beautiful and I will acknowledge it
Every chance I get, I don't like to hate

For me *loving* is just much more fun
If you truly *love Jesus*
Hate just isn't an option
Today, I ask you a question
Do you always tell family and friends how much
you miss them and *love* them?
The opportunity you get today might not come
again tomorrow

I had opportunities when I could of said
"I love you"
Instead I bickered and argued
Then I realized I wouldn't make that mistake again
From now on I will show genuine concern for the
needs of others
Loving is so important because we live in a world
where a lot of people are hurting and broken

One thing we must always remember is that *love*
and hate have always been opposites
You can't *love* while you hate and you can't hate
while you *love*
Except for when we *love* a sinner but hate their sin
Just like *Jesus* did when *He* died for us
Way back when
While we sinned
If we follow *His* example and stop worrying about
trying to change other people
Let's start by changing ourselves
By allowing *God's* Word to renew our minds
As well as looking at others with eyes of *love*
Because hatred only stirs up conflicts and strife
While *love* on the other hand covers a multitude of
offences
That's the only way we can make a difference
Then things can change

The definition of hate is to dislike someone or
something with a passion
Why waste our time hating when we can spend our
time passionately *loving*
Giving heartfelt hugs
Speaking words of *love* that lift others up
Instead of tearing people down
Especially because we have all hit rock bottom or
have been down and out

Waiting and hoping for someone to notice
How sad we feel deep inside no matter how
much we pretend or try to hide
Always remember that God counts your tears
And He sends His love through people that
with Him are connected
Today I say listen and obey God's word
Since it was He that said:
"Pray for your enemies and do good to those
that hate you"

How different from them are you if you only
do good to those that love you?

How many of you will accept the Love your
enemy challenge today?

Can you share the love of Christ with all that
God sends your way?
He says to LOVE one another just as
He has loved you
Always remember that the mind is the battlefield
And you don't know what confusing thoughts
Are swirling around in peoples heads
Causing disillusion, anxiety, hopelessness, loneliness,
depression and hate
We also don't know what they have suffered that
makes them act that way

Let's be that shoulder they can cry on
Or that friend they can actually count on
By being patient, kind and understanding
Not just telling them we *love* them with words
but showing them with our actions
Instead of always focusing on ourselves
Lets tune our ears to the needs of someone else

Most importantly
GOD is LOVE
Love is also an intense feeling of deep affection
If we truly know **Him** let's reflect **Him**
By choosing *love* over hate
Until we master the skill
of being selfless
Then everyday we'll become more like **Christ**
Finally
His word says that it is through *love* not hate
that we can conquer all.

Hebrews 13:20-21
"Now may the God of peace, who brought up from
the dead our Lord Jesus—the great Shepherd of the
sheep—with the blood of the everlasting covenant,
equip you with all that is good to do His will,
working in us what is pleasing in His sight, through
Jesus Christ. Glory belongs to Him forever and ever.
Amen."

Revelation 21:3-8

"Then I heard a loud voice from the throne:

Look! God's dwelling is with humanity,
and He will live with them.
They will be His people,
and God Himself will be with them
and be their God.
He will wipe away every tear from their eyes.
Death will no longer exist;
grief, crying, and pain will exist no longer,
because the previous things have passed away. Then
the One seated on the throne said, "Look! I am
making everything new." He also said, "Write,
because these words are faithful and true."
And He said to me, "It is done! I am the Alpha and
the Omega, the Beginning and the End. I will give
water as a gift to the thirsty from the spring of
life. The victor will inherit these things, and I will
be his God, and he will be My son. But the cowards,
unbelievers, vile, murderers, sexually immoral,
sorcerers, idolaters, and all liars—their share will
be in the lake that burns with fire and sulfur, which
is the second death."

Jesus Loves You!

Made in the USA
Las Vegas, NV
24 July 2023

75201152R00090